Comparative International Characteristics of Banking

James R. Barth
Auburn University and Milken Institute

Gerard Caprio, Jr.,
World Bank

Daniel E. Nolle
Office of the Comptroller of the Currency

OCC Economics Working Paper 2004-1

January 2004

The views expressed in this paper are those of the authors alone and not those of the Office of the Comptroller of the Currency or the U.S. Treasury Department, nor The World Bank, its management, the Executive Directors, nor the countries they represent. A version of this paper will appear in *A Companion to International Business Finance,* Raj Aggarwal (editor), Blackwell Publishing, Inc., Malden, Massachusetts (forthcoming). We wish to thank Gary Whalen for helpful comments, Cindy Lee for excellent research assistance, and Amy Millen for editorial assistance.

Please address correspondence to Daniel E. Nolle, Senior Financial Economist, Policy Analysis Division, Office of the Comptroller of the Currency, 250 E. Street, SW, Washington, DC 20219 (phone: 202-874-4442; e-mail: daniel.nolle@occ.treas.gov)

Comparative International Characteristics of Banking

James R. Barth, Gerard Caprio, Jr., and Daniel E. Nolle

Office of the Comptroller of the Currency
Economic and Policy Analysis Working Paper 2004-1

January 2004

Abstract: This paper compares key characteristics of banking systems across countries. A basic premise underlying our review is that the increasing globalization of banking and finance mandate a broad, cross-country perspective on banking issues. Indeed, cross-country comparisons can add insight into basic issues in banking that may not emerge, or are only partially discernible, from single-country analyses. With this in mind, we review representative research dealing with four fundamental aspects of international banking: the structure of banking, with emphasis on the connection between the development of the banking system and economic growth; banking industry performance; banking regulation, supervision, and corporate governance; and banking crises. We augment each of these discussions with an examination of the cross-country "landscape" of key dimensions of banking, using data for over 50 countries.

I. Introduction

Few would argue with the proposition that national policy makers, businesses, and analysts in countries everywhere must deepen their understanding and sharpen their awareness of foreign financial systems. The increased globalization and interconnectedness of business and finance provides one set of motives for this effort. In addition, there have been numerous banking and financial crises in the past two decades, and the effects of such crises have had wide-ranging repercussions around the world. Further, national policy discussion on banking and finance can benefit from an international perspective. International comparisons can reveal trends and norms that might be useful in debates about national banking and financial policies, and an awareness of banking and financial systems in other countries can promote the realization that national financial policies are likely to have an impact across borders.[1] This paper, which compares key characteristics of banking systems across countries, has been written with these ideas in mind.

Our focus on bank systems in particular flows from several considerations. Recent research has established that the development of the financial system is crucial for the development of the economy as a whole. For all countries, the banking system is an important component of the financial system; for many countries, especially developing countries, the banking system is the dominant component of the financial system. In addition, many have pointed to the special nature of banks as financial intermediaries that simultaneously extend credit and administer the payments system, and are the conduit for monetary policy. Further, researchers and national and international policy makers have focused on the banking industry as a key actor in causing, and preventing, financial and economic crises.

---

[1] Such awareness is of growing importance, given that 146 countries belong to the World Trade Organization (WTO) and are bound by the Annex on Financial Services, which took effect in 1999. See Alexander (2002) for a detailed discussion of issues arising under this arrangement.

Throughout this paper we outline significant banking issues that have been addressed by an appeal to cross-country comparisons, citing representative studies relevant to each issue.[2] Then we present and discuss data – some of it assembled here for the first time -- describing key facets of the international banking landscape relevant to these issues. The paper is organized as follows. Section II considers several important aspects of banking industry structure, including the relative size of banking industries, the degree of government and foreign ownership of banking, and the degree of market power in banking systems. Section III compares banking industry performance across countries. Section IV deals with several important aspects of the regulation and supervision of banks. These include the range of activities in which banks are permitted to engage; the structure, scope and independence of the supervisory system; the implementation of supervision; and deposit insurance schemes.[3] Section IV also investigates the corporate governance of banks, and presents cross-country comparisons of key aspects of this important dimension of banking. Section V briefly describes the incidences of banking crises around the world, and summarizes ideas about their causes and prevention. Section VI summarizes and concludes.

II. Structure of Banking: Cross-Country Comparisons

The financial development of the banking industry, the degree of government and foreign ownership of banks, and the concentration of economic power in the banking industry are all key

---

[2] For an excellent survey of important aspects of 170 international comparative banking studies, see Brown and Skully (2003).

[3] The two words "regulation" and "supervision" do not refer to the same concept or process. As Jordan (2001) states, "regulation refers to the rules or procedures that are designed to govern an industry's behavior. It is the prescriptions or boundaries imposed on the industry by legislators and regulatory bodies in an effort to 'direct' it....Supervision, on the other hand, is the monitoring or oversight function that takes place after the regulations have been passed. It ensures, among other things, that activities are conducted in accordance with those regulations."

dimensions of the structure of banking.[4] Since the development of several large cross-country

comparative data sets in the past decade, researchers have investigated possible links among

significant aspects of banking industry structure and economic growth, development, and

stability. This section summarizes recent representative cross-country studies on financial

development and the banking industry, government and foreign ownership of banking, and the

competitiveness of banking industries.

II.A. Financial Development and the Banking Industry

Prior to the 1990s, relatively little research was directed to the issues of whether and how

the financial system fostered economic growth.[5] The prevailing view was that economic growth

leads financial sector growth, which responded to the wider and deeper development of markets

for goods and services. However, within the last decade, a growing body of research has focused

on the possible positive causal connection between the development of the financial system and

overall economic development. This literature outlines several key ways in which financial

systems contribute to economic growth:

- Financial systems mobilize savings by offering savers a range of savings vehicles.

- Financial systems allocate savings by using expertise individual savers do not possess to ascertain potential borrower creditworthiness.

- Financial systems reduce risk to individual savers by diversifying pooled assets across many investment opportunities.

- Financial systems generate liquidity by allowing savers to readily access savings while at the same time financial intermediaries fund long-term projects.

---

[4] What constitutes a "bank" varies across countries. This issue is explored in detail in section IV.A. below.

[5] See Levine (1997), Kahn (2000), Khan and Senhdj (2000), Wachtel (2003), World Bank (2001), and Phumiwasana (2003) for surveys of the literature on the role of the financial system in economic growth. For a comprehensive survey of this literature as well as several other aspects of international comparisons of banking, see Brown and Skully (2003). These works and others point to a very limited pre-1990s literature on the subject, most particularly Goldsmith (1969) and McKinnon (1973). King and Levine (1993a and 1993b), Beck, Levine, and Loayza (2000), and others point to Joseph Schumpeter's insights in the early twentieth century as the intellectual antecedent to the recent literature on finance and growth.

- Financial intermediaries contribute to risk management by monitoring borrowers and managers of enterprises to which credit has been extended.

Researchers using cross-country data have begun to build a compelling case that financial sector development promotes economic growth, and much of this work focuses on the banking system. For example, King and Levine (1993a), using data for 80 countries for 1960-1989, find a significant positive relationship between several measures of financial development, including total credit extended to the private sector by banks, and economic growth. Their finding that the initial level of financial development in 1960 was a significant predictor of the subsequent average rate of growth over the next 29 years suggests a causal relationship between financial sector development and overall economic development.[6] More recently, Levine, Loayza and Beck (2000), using data for 74 countries, find that the exogenous component of financial intermediation is positively associated with economic growth. Also addressing the issue of causation, Rajan and Zingales (1998) used industry-level data for 41 countries in finding that industries more dependent on external financing tend to grow faster in countries with a higher level of financial system development, in which external financing – including credit extended by the banking sector – is easier to obtain. In a related vein, Demirgüç-Kunt and Maksimovic (2002) also use firm-level data across 40 countries to find that in more financially developed economies, a larger proportion of firms grew above the maximum rate of growth achievable by similar firms when they lacked access to external finance.

---

[6] For a critique of early-1990s studies on finance and growth, see Arestis and Demestriades (1997), which focuses on a number of thorny methodological difficulties to be overcome in order to establish causality between financial development and economic development. Note, nevertheless, that as Bonin and Wachtel (2003, p.1) observe, "A strong consensus has emerged in the last decade that well-functioning financial intermediaries have a significant impact on economic growth." Several single-country studies explore this issue. See, e.g., Bae, Kang, and Lim (2002) using Korean data; Ongena, Smith, and Michalsen (2003) using Norwegian data; and Gan (2003a) using Japanese data.

The precise nature of causation between financial sector development and economic development remains under debate, and there is ample room for further research.[7] Nevertheless, future research must encompass an understanding of the nature of differences across the globe in the relative sizes of the banking and overall financial sectors. Consistent with the overall purpose of this chapter, we illustrate comparative cross-country information on these factors in Table 1 and Figure 1. Table 1 groups 55 countries by income level into four categories. The far left-hand column gives a measure of the size of the banking system relative to the economy, using the ratio of banking system assets to GDP for every country; the average bank-assets-to-GDP ratio for each income group is also displayed. The second column from the left gives the rank of each country in terms of the relative size of the banking system. It is clear from the average bank assets-to-GDP ratio for each income group that, with a group average bank assets-to-GDP ratio of 343 percent, high income countries have larger, more developed banking systems compared with countries in the other income categories. This ratio tends to decline as income levels fall.[8]

There are some notable deviations from this pattern, including the United States, with a bank assets-to-GDP ratio of 66 percent. Taking into account not only the banking system, but also stock and bond markets, the U.S. has the largest financial system in the world. Hence, its relatively small bank assets-to-GDP ratio is not a reflection of an undeveloped banking system, but rather an indication of the relatively lower importance of the banking system compared with

---

[7] Note that the debate on causation between financial sector development and economic growth is not entirely resolved. See, for example, Wachtel (2003).

[8] The growth of electronic finance may add a substantial dimension to the finance-and-growth dynamic, as discussed in Claessens, Glaessner, and Klingebiel (2001, and 2002). In particular, they point to evidence suggesting that developing countries may be able to "leapfrog" past the development of some components of traditional financial services infrastructure by adopting online and remote delivery mechanisms for financial services. Both studies included detailed cross-country comparisons of e-finance. Though still at relatively modest levels in most countries, growth in some electronic delivery channels is significant across countries at different stages of economic development.

the stock and bond markets. Figure 1 illustrates the size of the banking system in selected

countries to the total financial system, measured as bank assets plus bond market assets and stock

market capitalization.[9] At 16 percent, the banking system in the U.S. is the smallest among

these countries in this relative sense. In contrast, Germany has a banking system that is roughly

four times as large in the same relative sense. It is for this reason that the U.S. is referred to as

having a capital-markets-based financial system and Germany a bank-based system.[10]

II.B. Ownership of Banking

The ownership of banks is a key structural characteristic of banking on which some of the

emergent cross-country banking literature has focused. Two facets in particular have received

attention: the degree of government vs. private sector ownership of banks and foreign vs.

domestic ownership of banks.

Following the international banking crises of the mid-to-late 1990s, analysts and policy-

makers developed a keen interest in the degree to which the government is involved in a banking

system. In general, government ownership of banks is likely to short-circuit market pressures on

banks to make credit extension and investment decisions based on economic assessments of risk

and return.[11] As a result, the likelihood of credit problems and poor profitability is typically

higher for government-owned banks, leading to lower overall economic growth and to a greater

likelihood of systemic banking problems.

---

[9] Relatively few countries are illustrated in Figure 1 because bond market data is not available for many countries. Note that a branch of the finance and growth literature has focused on whether the composition of the financial system – in particular, whether it is bank-based or capital-markets-based – matters for economic growth. See, e.g., Levine and Zervos (1998), Beck and Levine (2002), and Levine (2002). The emerging consensus from this literature is that: 1) the overall level of financial development matters, rather than the composition per se; and 2) that in any case, given the convergence of product offerings by banks and capital markets, the issue may be obviated by market developments over time.

[10] For a comprehensive analysis of how and why the composition of financial systems differs across countries, see Allen and Gale (2000).

[11] See, e.g., LaPorta, Lopez-de-Salinas, and Shleifer (2002), Wurgler (2000), Barth, Caprio, and Levine (2001a and 2003) and Barth, Brumbaugh, Ramesh, and Yago (1998).

Table 1 shows the extent of government ownership of banks in 55 countries, based upon the percent of bank assets that are government-owned. There is wide variation across the world in the extent of government ownership of banks, from 0 percent in about one-third of the countries, to 80 percent in one country, India. Looking at the average degree of government ownership across the four income groups, it is also clear that, at 11 percent, the wealthiest countries have the lowest percent of government ownership of banking, and the poorest countries have the highest government ownership average, at 36 percent. The difference between the government ownership percentage for high income countries and for low income countries is statistically significant.

In the wake of the international banking crises of the 1990s, research has focused on the role of foreign banks.[12] A growing number of studies have found evidence that foreign bank entry tends to benefit the host country, particularly in emerging markets.[13] Foreign bank entry may

- stimulate competition in the banking industry, leading to higher efficiency for domestic banks;
- result in improvements in the quality and accessibility to financial services for host country firms and individuals;[14]
- result in the transfer to domestic banks of improved banking skills and technology.
- enhance a country's access to international capital.
- lead to improvements in host country supervision and regulation, as suggested by Levine (1996) and Crystal, Dages, and Goldberg (2002).[15,16]

---

[12] Of course, research on the impact of foreign banks on the domestic economy preceded the banking crises of the 1990s. See, e.g., Goldberg and Saunders (1981) and Walter and Gray (1983).

[13] See, e.g., Claessens, Demirgüç-Kunt, and Huizinga (2001), Crystal, Dages, and Goldberg (2002), and Caprio and Honohan (2002).

[14] Demirgüç-Kunt, Levine, and Min (1999), using an indicator of foreign bank presence, find that the presence of foreign banks does indeed influence domestic bank efficiency.

The story has a number of complexities, however. Foreign banks may perform differently in economies at different income levels, and hence their overall impact on the host economy may vary. For example, Claessens, Demirgüç-Kunt, and Huizinga (2001) found that foreign banks outperform (and therefore may competitively stimulate) domestic banks in developing countries, but underperform home-country banks in developed countries.[17] In addition, Morgan and Strahan (2003) found that foreign bank entry can result in greater business cycle volatility. Because of the variety of effects from foreign bank entry, and its relatively high public policy profile, further research on it is warranted.

As with the issue of government ownership of banks, it is useful to review the cross-country landscape on the relative importance of foreign banking. Table 1 gives one measure of the presence of foreign banking across countries, using the percent of bank assets that are foreign owned. Foreign ownership of bank assets ranges widely, from 0 percent (Saudi Arabia) to 99 percent (New Zealand). Looking across country groups, upper-middle-income level countries stand out: at 37 percent, they have a significantly higher proportion of foreign ownership of bank assets compared to any of the other three groups. Interestingly, the high income countries show about the same average percent foreign ownership of bank assets as the low income countries.

---

[15] Crystal, Dages, and Goldberg (2002, p.1) suggest this may occur because the entry of foreign banks encourages "higher standards in auditing, accounting and disclosure, … [and] credit risk underwriting. In addition, the entry of foreign banks could affect the supervisory system within a country by an indirect route: foreign entry could result in the "importation" of supervision, due to the oversight that home country supervisors exercise.

[16] As Claessens, Glaessner, and Klingebiel (2001 and 2002) point out, with the emergence of electronic banking, foreign "entry" need not be accomplished through establishing a physical presence. Although cross-border e-banking – where a bank located in a particular "home" country offers services to "host" country customers via, for example, the Internet – is still relatively rare, its potential is significant enough to have caused the Basel Committee on Bank Supervision to produce risk management documents on the issue. See Basel Committee (2002).

[17] This second finding is consistent with some single-country studies of foreign banks. See, e.g., DeYoung and Nolle (1996).

Overall, the data do not reveal a simple relationship between country income level and degree of foreign ownership of banking assets.

II.C. Competition in Banking

A key aspect of banking structure that has received a good deal of attention traditionally in single-country studies is the degree of competition in banking. Recently, there has been a growing interest in cross-country comparisons of competition in banking.[18] Much of this work has focused on the effects of concentration. This is in response in part to the traditional structure-performance research originating in industrial organization theory and subsequently transferred over to single-country studies of banking that emphasized the concentration ratio as a key variable in explaining industry performance. But, as most recent research admits, concentration ratios (of bank assets or deposits) are not necessarily the best measure of the degree of competitiveness in a banking industry.[19] A few studies have tried to gauge the contestability of banking markets across countries,[20] but most recent comparative international research has used data on concentration ratios, albeit with reservations, because reliable cross-country data is now widely available.

This new body of research has recognized that concentration in banking may play a more complex role than traditionally hypothesized for nonfinancial industries.[21] For example, with respect to the pricing and availability of banking services -- which in turn affect economic

---

[18] See Claessens and Laeven (2003) and Cetorelli (2003) for surveys of recent research on this topic.

[19] See Claessens and Laeven (2003) for an example of this point.

[20] Claessens and Laeven (2003) is a noteworthy recent example.

[21] Allen and Gale (2003) emphasize this point. Note that industrial organization theory has long recognized that the relationship between industry concentration and performance is far from clear-cut. See, e.g., the famous survey by Weiss (1974).

growth and development -- concentrated banking markets could lead to less lending at higher costs to borrowers, especially smaller firms, which in turn has negative effects on economic growth and development.[22] However, as Rajan (1992), Cetorelli (2003), Claessens and Laeven (2003) and others have pointed out, the higher the market power, the more likely are banks to invest in information gathering about firms. The reasons for this are that they are more likely to be of sufficient size to gather and process relatively costly-to-obtain information about opaque firms, and because they are more likely to be able to enjoy monopoly rents from having done so. As a consequence, high concentration could lead to greater access to credit for firms, and hence improved economic growth and development.

The empirical evidence is mixed, however. Bikker and Groeneveld (2000), for example, found negative effects for concentration on banking industry competitiveness in the European Union, while Claessens and Laeven (2003) found "no evidence that banking system concentration negatively relates to competitiveness."[23] Beck, Demirgüç-Kunt, and Maksimovic (2003) found a complex relationship between bank concentration and access to external finance: concentration increases obstacles to financing and therefore decreases the likelihood of firms receiving bank financing, a result that grows weaker as firm size increases. However, they also found that this relationship fades in countries with good contract enforcement, an emphasis on the rule of law, low corruption, and good corporate governance. In addition, higher levels of economic and financial sector development, and a larger share of foreign banks reduce the negative impacts of high concentration, while a larger share of government ownership of banks

---

[22] Cetorelli (2003) lists several recent theoretical studies supporting this hypothesis.

[23] Claessens and Laeven (2003), p. 35.

and higher restrictions on permissible activities for banks enhances the deleterious effects of concentration.

There is also controversy in the relatively small amount of research on the relationship between bank concentration and financial system stability.[24] On the one hand, as Allen and Gale (2003) have pointed out, less concentrated banking systems with many small banks may be more prone to crises than a concentrated banking industry with a few large banks, which may be able to diversify risks better. In addition, a few large banks may enjoy higher profits and therefore have a cushion against adverse shocks as compared to a system with many small banks.[25] Further, it may be easier for regulators and shareholders to monitor a few large banks, as compared to a system of many small banks. On the other hand, a system with a few large dominant banks may be more prone to crisis if such large banks operate under a "too-big-to-fail" policy that encourages moral hazard behavior. In addition, large banks also tend to be more complex than smaller banks, and hence may be more, not less, difficult for regulators and shareholders to monitor. Finally, banks with greater market power may tend to charge higher prices for banking services, which may induce client firms to assume greater risks in order to recoup expenditures.[26] In their empirical investigation of the relationship between concentration and financial stability in 79 countries, Beck, Demirgüç-Kunt, and Levine (2003) found that crises are less likely in more concentrated banking systems.

---

[24] See Beck, Demirgüç-Kunt, and Levine (2003) for an insightful synopsis of this literature.

[25] Theoretical research in this vein includes Gan (2003b), Hellman, Murdock, and Stiglitz (2000), Keeley (1990), and Marcus (1984). Gan (2003c) provides empirical evidence of a link between market structure and financial stability, using data on the Texas real estate crisis in the 1980s.

[26] Beck, Demirgüç-Kunt, and Levine (2003) point to a recent study by Boyd and De Nicoló (2003) for this hypothesis.

Given the controversy that surrounds the issue of competitiveness of the banking industry and its impact on the economy, as well as the recent vintage of the still relatively small amount of analysis, more research is warranted. It is also useful to consider relevant information on the competitive banking landscape across countries. Table 1 provides two measures of banking competitiveness. The first is the 3-bank concentration ratio, measuring the percent of banking system assets held by the top three banks. As Table 1 illustrates, this ratio varies widely across countries, from a high of 97 percent in Finland to a low of 16 percent in the United Kingdom. Looking at the average value of the concentration ratio for each of the four income groups of countries, there does not appear to be much variation, with each group close to the overall average of 51 percent. As a consequence, no simple pattern appears to exist between concentration and the level of economic development.

Another measure of market power that is sometimes used is net interest margins, under the reasoning that the greater the degree of competition in a banking system, the lower will be the spread between the interest rates banks charge their customers and their own interest expenses.[27] Table 1 also presents net interest margins as a percent of total assets across countries. As with the 3-bank concentration ratio, figures vary widely across countries, with lower margins indicating less market power in the banking system.[28] Unlike the case of the concentration ratio, however, there appears to be a pattern in the relationship between the level

---

[27] But see Demirgüç-Kunt, Laeven, and Levine (2003) for a number of complicating factors surrounding this reasoning. Note also that net interest margins can be interpreted as a gauge of the degree of efficiency in the banking industry, under the related reasoning that in a more competitive banking system the drive for efficiencies will squeeze margins.

[28] Obviously this measure, as well as any other single measure, must be viewed cautiously. For example, the low figure in Table 1 is –3.84 for Indonesia, certainly more a reflection of that system's banking crisis than a solid measure of relative market power.

of economic development (as represented by income level) and average net interest margins. In particular, the higher the level of economic development, the lower is market power in banking.

III. Performance of Banks: Cross-Country Comparisons

As with banking structure, there are noteworthy differences across countries in banking industry performance. Table 2 shows several measures of banking performance across 55 countries using data for 1999. Two measures of bank profitability are included: return on assets (ROA) and return on equity (ROE). Both measures show wide variation across countries, and although they do not necessarily run in tandem, countries stand in roughly the same position relative to each other by either measure.[29] Looking at the averages for the four income level groups, a clear-cut positive correlation exists between ROE and income level. The pattern is not as clear in the case of ROA, although the two highest income groups show a considerably greater average ROA than the two lowest.

Single-country studies of bank profitability have focused on bank-specific variables as key determinants.[30] As large-scale cross-country databases have recently been developed, researchers have investigated determinants of bank profitability going beyond the rather narrow set of explanatory variables used in single-country studies. Demirgüç-Kunt and Huizinga (1999) is representative of this newer approach. That study of more than 5000 banks in 80 countries over the 1988-95 period, found that in addition to bank-specific factors, such as the equity-to-assets and loans-to-assets ratios, macroeconomic conditions (especially the level of economic

---

[29] These gauges of profitability do not always run in tandem, because a bank with a higher equity ratio will tend to have a higher ROA and a lower ROE than a bank with a lower equity ratio. As Demirgüç-Kunt and Huizinga (1999) point out, in some developing countries banks operate with very low equity capital, in part because there may be implicit government guarantees, and as a consequence their ROEs are high but do not reflect bank soundness.

[30] Although as Barth, Nolle, and Rice (1997) note, there does not seem to be a strong consensus on what constitutes the "core" model for explaining bank profitability.

development), deposit insurance regulation; degree of foreign ownership; and legal and institutional factors, such as the effectiveness of contract enforcement, all play a role in explaining (pre-tax) ROA. Subsequent studies, such as Demirgüç-Kunt and Huizinga (2001) that focused on the role of financial structure, and Barth, Nolle, Phumiwasana, and Yago (2003) that focused on the role of banking system supervisory structure, scope, and independence, broadly ratified these findings and offered extensions of the determinants of bank profitability by appealing to cross-country data sets.

Another gauge of bank performance illustrated in Table 2 is the ratio of noninterest revenue to total revenue. This ratio gives a measure of the degree to which a bank relies on noninterest-bearing, fee-generating activities relative to "traditional" interest-bearing activities, such as commercial and real estate loans. It may be a rough proxy for the degree of innovation in which banks are willing to engage, and/or a measure of their ability to diversify risks.[31] Consistent with this interpretation, the ratio of noninterest revenue to total revenue is much higher for the high income countries on average than for the other country income groups. On the other hand, consistent with Demirgüç-Kunt and Huizinga (1999), who found that a relatively high ratio of noninterest earning assets had a negative impact on profitability, Table 2 shows that the lowest income group of countries has a relatively high ratio of noninterest revenue to total revenue. It is possible, therefore, that this variable captures different dynamics for developed compared with developing countries.[32]

Table 2 also displays data across countries for a standard measure of credit quality – nonperforming loans to total loans. Despite the fact that countries use different accounting and

---

[31] On the former point, see Furst, Lang, and Nolle (2002); on the latter point, see Stiroh (2002).

[32] One possibility is that a large proportion of noninterest revenue may be accounted for by deposit charges and similar fees which are directly tied to "traditional" interest-bearing services, and hence are not reflective of product diversification. The authors thank Gary Whalen for this insight.

regulatory standards for classifying impaired loans with, in general, the less developed countries using less rigorous standards, there is a clear-cut negative pattern between income level groups and nonperforming loans to total loans. This is consistent with other gauges of bank performance showing overall weaker banking systems in less developed countries.

A final important dimension of bank performance meriting attention is efficiency. The comprehensive and oft-cited survey of bank efficiency studies by Berger and Humphrey (1997) included only six cross-country studies. There are significant difficulties even in single-country studies of bank efficiency in measuring both inputs and outputs in banking, making estimation of efficiency difficult; these problems are magnified for cross-country studies where such inputs and outputs data as exist are not standardized across countries.[33] Nevertheless, the gap in cross-country analyses and comparisons of bank efficiency has begun to be addressed, as noted, for example in Brown and Skully (2003). Although it is perhaps too early to point to the kind of "stylized facts" that have emerged from cross-country banking studies in other respects, it is possible to get a rough idea of what the cross-country landscape may resemble. Table 1 includes information across countries on net interest margins, which are commonly regarded as indicative of overall banking efficiency, under the argument that in more efficient banking systems the gap between the rates banks receive on, and pay for, funds will be relatively small because of competitive pressures.[34] In the event, the country income group averages show that higher income countries have lower net interest margins, consistent with the expectation of more efficient banking in more developed countries.

---

[33] See Brown and Skully (2003) for a concise explanation of these data and methodological problems.

[34] See, e.g., Demirgüç-Kunt and Huizinga (1999).

IV. Regulation, Supervision, and Corporate Governance of Banking

The banking industry is regarded as being different from other industries. The reasoning for regarding banks as "special" was aptly summarized by Corrigan (1982), who argued that banks:

- provide transactions services and administer the payments system;

- supply backup liquidity;

- are the conduit through which monetary policy is administered.

Consequently, a systemic crisis in the banking system can spread throughout the economy. Many have argued that contagion and systemic problems are more common in banking than in other sectors. In light of this, all governments regulate and supervise banks, although regulatory and supervisory approaches and measures differ across countries.[35]

This section compares the regulation, supervision, and corporate governance of banks across countries, focusing on several significant aspects and issues surrounding these dimensions of regulation and supervision. Examined across countries are:

- the range of activities in which banks are permitted to engage;

- the way in which banking supervision is structured, the scope of the authority of banking supervisors, and their relative independence from political and other influences;

- differences in the implementation of supervision;

- deposit insurance systems;

- the nature of corporate governance in banking systems.

---

[35] As noted earlier, "regulation" refers to the set of laws and rules applicable to banking, and "supervision" is defined as the monitoring by authorities of banks' activities and the enforcement of banking regulations. Barth, Nolle, Phumiwasana, and Yago (2003, p. 70, footnote 7) refer to a line of reasoning that has been developed explaining why banks should not be regulated.

IV.A. Regulation: Permissible Activities for Banks

The banking industry is regulated and supervised in every country, but wide differences separate the activities in which banks are permitted to engage. Some countries restrict banks to a narrow range of activities, whereas others allow them to engage in a broad array. Since it is the scope of activities that essentially defines the term "bank," a bank is therefore not the same in every country around the world.[36] It is the regulatory authorities, moreover, that not only determine the extent to which the activities of banks differ across countries, but also the extent to which they differ from nonbank-financial and nonfinancial firms within countries.

Table 3 presents information on the differences in permissible activities for banks in countries grouped by income level. The activities include the ability of banks to engage in the business of securities underwriting, brokering, and dealing; insurance underwriting and selling; and real estate investment, development, and management. Permissible activities also include the degree to which banks may own nonfinancial firms and vice versa. The degree to which these activities are restricted are denoted by the terms unrestricted, permitted, restricted and prohibited. These designations are based upon Barth, Caprio and Levine (2001b), with each country's regulations concerning each of these activities rated on the degree of restrictiveness from 1 to 4.[37] These numbers correspond to the four designations, unrestricted through

---

[36] For an interesting discussion of the evolution of the legal definition of a bank in the U.S., see Haubrich and Santos (2003, pp.147-148). In a similar vein, there is the issue as to what is meant by the term "banking product." To a growing extent product convergence is occurring, in which similar financial products are offered by different financial service industries. The regulatory and supervisory issue is that those products may in effect receive different regulatory treatment because they are being offered from differently regulated industries. For example, there is a growing similarity between performance standby letters of credit typically issued by banks, and surety bonds typically issued by insurance firms.

[37] More specifically, unrestricted means a full range of activities can be conducted in the bank; permitted means a full range of activities can be conducted, but some or all must be conducted in subsidiaries; restricted means less than a full range of activities can be conducted in the bank or subsidiaries; prohibited means the activity cannot be conducted in either the bank or subsidiaries. For bank ownership of nonfinancial firms: unrestricted means a bank may own 100 percent of the equity in any nonfinancial firm; permitted means a bank may own 100 percent of the equity in a nonfinancial firm, but ownership is limited based on a bank's equity capital; restricted means a bank can

prohibited, with the higher number indicating greater restrictiveness. This approach enables one

to construct a narrow index of activities restrictiveness (i.e., securities, insurance, and real estate)

as well as an overall restrictiveness index (i.e., the activities restrictiveness plus the

restrictiveness of bank ownership of nonfinancial firms and vice versa). The narrow index may

range in value from 3 to 12, while the overall index may range in value from 5 to 20.[38]

Table 3 shows that securities activities are the least restricted and real estate activities are

the most restricted in countries across all income levels. Indeed, not a single country prohibits

banks from engaging in securities activities. In contrast, one-fourth of the 55 countries prohibit

them from engaging in real estate activities. Although no country prohibits all three activities,

Mauritius comes the closest by prohibiting banks from engaging in insurance and real estate

activities and restricting their securities activities. India is interesting because it also prohibits

insurance and real estate activities for banks yet allows them unrestricted securities activities. At

the other end of the restrictiveness spectrum, three countries grant banks unrestricted securities,

insurance, and real estate powers – Germany, New Zealand, and Switzerland. Recently, a few

countries have become more liberal in granting banks broader powers. The U.S., for example,

with the enactment of the Gramm-Leach-Bliley Act (GLBA) in late 1999, now permits rather

than restricts banks' access to both securities and insurance activities.[39]

The degree of restrictiveness on the mixing of banking and commerce also displays

substantial variation across countries. Bank ownership of nonfinancial firms is more restricted

---

only acquire less than 100 percent of the equity in a nonfinancial firm; prohibited means a bank may not acquire any equity investment in a nonfinancial firm. For nonfinancial firm ownership of banks: unrestricted means a nonfinancial firm may own 100 percent of the equity in a bank; permitted means unrestricted, but need prior authorization or approval; restricted means limits are placed on ownership, such as a maximum percentage of a bank's capital or shares; prohibited means no equity investment in a bank is allowed.

[38] The simple correlation between these two indexes is a positive and statistically significant 0.91.

[39] See Barth, Brumbaugh, and Wilcox (2000). Note that the data for Table 3 was collected pre-GLBA.

than nonfinancial firm ownership of banks. Only 15 percent of the countries allow banks unrestricted ownership of nonfinancial firms, whereas 40 percent allow unrestricted ownership of banks by nonfinancial firms. Table 3 shows that no country prohibits the mixing of banking and commerce.[40]

Based on the index of overall restrictiveness, the least restrictive country is New Zealand, while Japan, Mauritius, and El Salvador are tied for being the most restrictive. More generally, there is a tendency for high income countries to be less restrictive than countries in the three other income groups. Specifically, the value of the narrow index of activities restrictiveness is statistically significantly lower for high income countries than the other three groupings. The value of the overall index is also statistically significantly lower for the high income countries than the upper and lower middle income countries, but not for the low income countries.

Despite the differences among countries in the regulatory treatment of permissible activities for banks, the ultimate goal of bank regulation and supervision is to promote systemic stability. Additionally, regulation and supervision may also be aimed at promoting the development and efficiency of the banking sector. The important issue is what mix of permissible activities is best for banks in each country around the world to achieve these goals. At the theoretical level, there are arguments on both sides of the issue. The main reasons for restricting the permissible activities of banks are as follows. First, conflicts of interest may arise when banks are allowed to engage in a diverse group of activities.[41] Second, banks will have more opportunities to increase risk when allowed to engage in a broader range of activities,

---

[40] As a result of GLBA, however, the U.S. in some respects has tightened restrictions on the mixing of banking and commerce.

[41] See, e.g., Edwards (1979) and John, John and Saunders (1994).

which they are more likely to do when they have access to deposit insurance.[42] Third, the wider

the range of activities, the greater the formation of financial conglomerates that may be

extraordinarily difficult to supervise.[43] Fourth, large institutions may become so politically and

economically powerful that they become "too big to discipline." Lastly, the creation of financial

conglomerates may reduce competition and thus efficiency in the financial sector.

There are theoretical reasons, however, for allowing banks to engage in a broad range of

activities. Fewer regulatory restrictions on the activities of banks may:

- permit the exploitation of economies of scale and scope in gathering and processing information about firms, managing different types of risk for customers, advertising and distributing financial services, enforcing contracts, and building reputational capital with clients;

- increase the franchise value of banks and thereby enhance their incentive to behave prudently;

- lead to diversified income streams and thus create more stable banks;

- limit the ability of the government to use banks to allocate funds to less productive projects, and thereby promote bank performance and stability.[44]

Although existing empirical studies do not fully resolve these theoretical debates, most of

the literature suggests there are positive benefits from permitting banks broad powers. For

instance, Berger and Udell (1996), DeLong (1991) and Ramirez (1995, 2002) find that expanded

banking powers are associated with a lower cost of capital and less stringent cash-flow

constraints. Vander Vennet (1999), moreover, finds that unrestricted banks have higher levels of

operational efficiency than banks with more restricted powers. In terms of diversification,

---

[42] See, e.g., Boyd, Change and Smith (1998).

[43] Michael Camdessus (1997), e.g., remarked that we are witnessing "...the organization of financial conglomerates, whose scope is often hard to grasp and whose operations may be impossible for outside observers -- even bank supervisors -- to monitor."

[44] Saunders (1994) provides a good review that focuses specifically on the potential benefits and costs of mixing banking and commerce.

Eisenbeis and Wall (1984) and Kwan and Laderman (1999) argue that because profits from providing different financial services are not highly correlated, there are diversification benefits from allowing broader powers. Furthermore, Ang and Richardson (1994), Kroszner and Rajan (1994), Puri (1996), and Ramirez (1995) find that broad banks did not systemically abuse their powers in the pre-Glass-Steagall days of the U.S. Gande, Puri and Saunders (1999), moreover, find that allowing banks' securities powers enhances competition.

Drawing upon a comprehensive cross-country dataset, Barth, Caprio and Levine (2001a) find that greater regulatory restrictions are associated with: (1) a higher probability of a country suffering a major banking crisis, and (2) lower banking-sector efficiency. They found no countervailing positive effects from restricting banking-sector activities. Regulatory restrictions, for example, were not closely associated with less concentration, more competition, or greater securities-market development.

More recently, Barth, Caprio, and Levine (2003) examine a much larger group of countries and find that restricting bank activities is negatively associated with bank performance and stability, as compared to when banks can diversify into other financial activities. Although theory provides conflicting predictions about the implications of restricting the range of bank activities, the results are consistent with the view that broad banking powers allow banks to diversify income sources and enhance stability. Their finding, moreover, is not due to reverse causality.[45] Furthermore, extending their earlier study, they control for official supervisory practices, capital regulations, regulations on competition, government ownership of banks, and the moral hazard engendered by generous deposit insurance schemes. The negative relationship between restricting bank activities and bank development and stability therefore does not seem to

---

[45] See Barth, Caprio, and Levine (2001a) for a discussion of this issue.

be because of an obvious omitted variable. Furthermore, they find no evidence that restricting

bank activities produces positive results in particular institutional or policy environments.

Specifically, they do not find improvements in bank performance or stability from restrictions on

bank activities in economies that offer more generous deposit insurance, have weak official

supervision, ineffective incentives for private monitoring, or that lack stringent capital standards.

IV.B. Supervision: Structure, Scope, and Independence

Banking crises, rapid structural change, and the continuing globalization of banking have

led national and multilateral policy makers to focus increased attention on the crucial role of

banking supervision. This focus is reinforced by the fact that "…one of the important

[international] trends has been, and continues to be, a move away from regulation and towards

supervision."[46] Policy discussions specifically focus on several issues that must be addressed in

establishing and maintaining effective supervision, including the structure, scope, and

independence of bank supervision. Should banks be subject to one or multiple supervisory

authorities? Should the central bank be involved in bank supervision? Should bank supervisory

authorities supervise other financial service industries, including in particular securities and

insurance? To what degree should bank supervisors be subject to political and economic policy

pressure and influence? How these issues are addressed is important because policies that fail to

provide for an appropriate bank supervisory framework may undermine bank performance and

even lead to full-scale banking crises.

The intense interest policy makers have shown in these issues has not been reflected in

research, in part because of data limitations. In particular, little systematic empirical evidence

exists on how, or indeed whether, the structure, scope, and independence of bank supervision

---

[46]Crockett (2001).

affect the banking industry. One recent study addressing this gap is Barth, Nolle, Phumiwasana, and Yago (2003).[47] That study summarizes the policy debates surrounding these issues, drawing on a growing conceptual literature. It also examines whether and how the structure, scope, and independence of banking supervision affect a key dimension of bank performance – bank profitability. The results indicate, at most, a weak influence for the structure of supervision on a particular dimension of bank performance.

A key policy decision in designing the structure of the bank supervisory system is whether there should be a single bank supervisory authority or multiple supervisors. Although previous conceptual literature covers a number of possible advantages and disadvantages to each option, perhaps the strongest reason for some to advocate a single supervisory authority is because they fear a "competition in laxity" between multiple supervisors, while those who favor a system with two or more bank supervisors stress the benefits of a "competition in ideas" among multiple supervisors.[48]

One essential set of information largely missing from the previous literature on the issue of the structure of supervision is what different countries around the world have chosen to do, perhaps reflecting the view that as with financial systems themselves, there may be many roads to an adequate system. Table 5 provides information on the international "landscape" of bank supervisory structure. The vast majority of countries have a single bank supervisory authority. Nevertheless, 16 percent of the 55 countries, including the U.S., assign banking supervision to

---

[47] Martinez and Rose (2003) address the issue of "integrated" supervision of banking and securities firms and/or insurance firms using results from a survey of 15 countries with such systems.

[48] See Barth, Nolle, Phumiwasana, and Yago (2003, pp. 70-73) for a detailed discussion of the advantages and disadvantages of single supervisor and multiple supervisors systems of bank regulation. Also, see Barth, Dopico, Nolle and Wilcox (2002).

multiple supervisory authorities. There is no systematic pattern to the division between single and multiple supervisory regimes across geographical regions or country income levels.[49]

Countries must also decide whether to assign responsibility for bank supervision to the central bank. As with the issue of single or multiple bank supervisors, the conceptual literature is split on the relative advantages and disadvantages of the central bank being a bank supervisor.[50] Perhaps the most strongly emphasized argument in favor of assigning supervisory responsibility to the central bank is that as a bank supervisor, the central bank will have first-hand knowledge of the condition and performance of banks. This in turn can help it identify and respond to the emergence of a systemic problem in a timely manner. Those pointing to the disadvantages of assigning bank supervision to the central bank stress the inherent conflict of interest between supervisory responsibilities and responsibility for monetary policy. The conflict could become particularly acute during an economic downturn, in that the central bank may be tempted to pursue a too-loose monetary policy to avoid adverse effects on bank earnings and credit quality, and/or encourage banks to extend credit more liberally than warranted based on credit quality conditions to complement an expansionary monetary policy.

As with the single-multiple supervisor debate, a useful first step in addressing the debate over the bank supervisory role of the central bank is to ascertain basic facts. Table 4 compares the bank supervisory role of the central bank in 55 countries. Almost two-thirds of those countries assign banking supervision to the central bank, including 53 percent in which the central bank is the single bank supervisory authority. Like the U.S., a few countries (13 percent

---

[49] Briault (1999, pp.15-16) briefly discusses the issue of a transnational financial services supervisor. See also the discussion in the *Economist* (2002). Transnational issues also come into play in the debate over financial supervision in the European Union. See, e.g., Lannoo (2000), and International Monetary Fund (2001), Goodhart (2002), and Schüler (2003).

[50] See Barth, Nolle, Phumiwasana, and Yago (2003, pp.73-76) for a detailed discussion of this literature.

25

of the total) give bank supervisory authority to the central bank and at least one other agency (i.e., have a multiple supervisory system, and assign bank supervisory authority to the central bank).

Much of the discussion about consolidating financial services supervision takes as its starting point the observation that financial service companies are growing increasingly complex. Financial conglomerates that operate in the banking, securities, and insurance industries are among the most powerful corporations in many countries. Some have argued that a supervisor with broad scope to cover all financial services is necessary to supervise such entities effectively and, in particular, to insure that supervisory oversight of risk management by such conglomerates is not fragmented, uncoordinated, or incomplete. The most significant argument against a supervisory authority with broad scope is that it would result in an undue concentration of power that would otherwise be dispersed among several agencies. This could increase the likelihood of regulatory capture and retard financial innovation.[51]

Table 4 presents an international comparison of the scope of supervision across countries. In the majority of countries (58 percent) the authority responsible for bank supervision is confined only the banking industry. However, bank supervisory authorities also supervise securities firms in 13 percent of the countries, and insurance firms in 11 percent of the countries. In 8 countries (15 percent), the authority(ies) responsible for bank supervision also supervises both securities and insurance firms.

A third bank supervision issue has begun to receive far greater attention from researchers in the wake of numerous recent and costly banking and currency crises. Consensus is arising from the burgeoning research on the causes of banking and currency crises that independence for

---

[51] See Barth, Nolle, Phumiwasana, and Yago (2003) for a detailed discussion of this issue.

supervisory authorities is crucial for well-functioning banks and for financial system stability.[52]

Supervisors are "independent" to the extent that they are insulated from, or able to resist, pressure and influence to modify supervisory practices in order to advance a policy agenda that is at odds with the maintenance of a safe and sound banking system. Supervisory independence allows bank supervisors to monitor the financial condition of banks in a strictly professional and consistent fashion. In addition, it allows them to elicit the appropriate level of responsiveness to the guidance, constructive criticism, and direction they give to banks. In essence, supervisory independence makes it possible for supervisors to "call it like they see it" and to have their advice and orders heeded.

Using information from the World Bank as described in Barth, Caprio and Levine (2001b), Barth, Nolle, Phumiwasana, and Yago (2003) construct an index of the degree of independence bank supervisors possess. The index, with values from 1 (low independence) to 3 (high independence), was based on supervisory authorities' answers to a series of questions designed to ascertain how insulated the supervisor is from political pressure. Table 4 displays how 55 countries ranked according to this index. Forty-four percent of the countries have bank supervisory authorities with relatively low independence, while more than one-quarter (27 percent) have relatively high independence; 29 percent of the countries rank in between. Although countries with low supervisory independence are scattered across country income

---

[52]As Barth, Nolle, Phumiwasana, and Yago (2003) point out, the issue of independence for supervisory authorities has also attracted increasing attention among policy makers. In particular, the Basel Committee's 1997 *Core Principles for Effective Banking Supervision* highlights supervisory independence. The *Core Principles* comprise 25 basic principles that must be in place for a supervisory system to be effective. The principles cover licensing, prudential regulations and requirements, methods of supervision, information requirements, formal powers of supervisory authorities, and cross-border banking. Importantly, the first principle outlines necessary "preconditions for effective banking supervision," and chief among these fundamental preconditions is that agencies responsible for banking supervision "should possess operational independence" (*Core Principles*, p. 4).

groups, only two "High Independence" countries appear in the lower middle income group, and none in the low income group.

The World Bank (2001) also addresses another aspect of independence, namely the extent to which supervisors are protected from criminal or civil prosecution for the performance of their duties. In effect, supervisees not only can employ the political process to reduce the extent to which their activities are subject to official oversight, but they can also use the courts. If supervisors enjoy a low level of compensation, which is often associated with a low degree of political independence, and simultaneously face the unprotected threat of large civil penalties for conducting vigorous supervision, then supervisory oversight can be expected to be weak. However research in this area is still in its infancy.

IV.C. Implementation of Supervision

The debate no doubt will continue on the relative advantages and disadvantages of different supervisory system structures. However, as important as that debate is, it is secondary to issues surrounding the implementation of supervision. In this regard, we can make a number of comparisons on the nature of scope of supervisory practices based upon World Bank data. In particular, Table 5 shows comparative information for several aspects of the implementation of supervision across 55 countries.

First, Table 5 presents information on the frequency of on-site bank examinations. We have no direct information on the scope of bank examinations across our sample of countries – i.e., what aspects of bank operations are examined, and how thoroughly. However, in about half of the countries' bank supervisors perform an on-site examination of most banks annually. On the other hand, many countries perform on-site bank examinations less frequently, and some countries, for example the United Kingdom, rely heavily on "off-site" examination of information submitted by banks to supervisory authorities.

Another way to measure the nature of supervisory implementation is to gauge supervisory resource utilization. A crude measure is to calculate the average number of supervisors on a per-bank basis, as is illustrated in the middle column of Table 5. By this measure, while the three lower country income groups are roughly similar, the high income countries show a much lower supervisors-per-bank ratio. The number of banks in each country will influence this measure heavily. The high income countries, with much larger economies on average than the lower income countries, tend to have many more banks on average than the lower income countries. An alternative measure of supervisory resource use is given in the far right-hand column of Table 5. "Banking Assets per Supervisory Staff" gives a rough measure of the "coverage" of banking system activity for which each supervisory staff member is responsible. Again, although there is wide variation across countries, a basic country income level pattern stands out. In particular, the "coverage" of banking activities on a per-staff-member basis is much higher for the high income countries than for the lower three income groups.[53]

IV.D. Deposit Insurance

The inherent fragility of banks has motivated a number of nations to establish deposit insurance schemes. Such schemes are intended to assure depositors that their funds are safe by having the government guarantee that they can always be withdrawn on demand at full value. To the extent that depositors believe that the government is able and willing to keep its promise, they will have no incentive to engage in widespread runs to withdraw their funds from banks.

---

[53] Goodhart, Schoenmaker, and Dasgupta (2002) consider an additional dimension of supervisory resources. Using a database for 91 countries, they examine the impact on bank supervisory posture that the mix of skills has, focusing in particular on the relative proportions of economists and lawyers.

By increasing depositor confidence, deposit insurance thus has the potential to provide for a more stable banking system.[54]

At the same time that deposit insurance increases depositor confidence, it creates a potentially serious "moral hazard" problem. When depositors believe that their funds are safe they have little, if any, incentive to monitor and police the activities of banks. When this type of depositor discipline is removed, banks are freer to engage in riskier activities. To the extent that this type of behavior is not kept in check once a country establishes a deposit insurance scheme, its banking system may still be susceptible to a crisis.

Under these circumstances, the establishment of a deposit insurance scheme is not a panacea. It provides both potential benefits and costs to a society. The challenge is to maximize the benefits while simultaneously minimizing the costs. For this reason, a better appreciation and understanding of deposit insurance is needed by governments and citizens in countries around the globe, particularly because ever more countries have been establishing such schemes in recent years. [55] Indeed, since the first national deposit insurance scheme was established by the United States in 1933, nearly 70 more countries have followed suit, most within the past 20 years.

There is widespread agreement that appropriate regulation and supervision are particularly important for preventing banking problems once countries have established a deposit insurance scheme. Those countries must increasingly contain the incentive for banks to engage in excessively risky activities once banks have access to deposits insured by the government. For, as Hovakimian, Kane and Laeven (2002), p.23) put it: "weaknesses in risk control can generate large fiscal and social costs under an explicit insurance regime, a truth that most recent

---

[54] See the seminal paper by Diamond and Dybvig (1983).

[55] In this regard, see the recent and excellent studies by Kane (2000) and Demirgüç-Kunt and Kane (2002).

financial crises underscore." The difficult task, however, is to replace the reduced discipline of the private sector with that of the government. Nonetheless, it has done with varying degrees of success in countries around the world. The proper way to do so involves both prudential regulations and effective supervisory practices.

Skilled supervisors and appropriate regulations can help prevent banks from taking on undue risk, and thereby exposing the insurance fund to excessive loses. At the same time, however, banks must not be so tightly regulated and supervised that they are prevented from adapting to a changing financial marketplace. If this happens, banks will be less able to compete and thus more likely to fail. The regulatory and supervisory authorities must therefore strike an appropriate balance between being too lenient and too restrictive in order to promote a safe and sound banking industry.

The appropriateness of specific regulations and supervisory practices depends upon the specific design features of a deposit insurance scheme. Some features may exacerbate moral hazard, whereas others may minimize it. Therefore a government must realize that when designing a scheme one must consider the effects of various features on both depositor confidence and moral hazard. In this regard, information has recently become available describing many of the important differences among deposit insurance schemes that have been established in a wide cross-section of countries. It is therefore useful to examine this "menu of deposit insurance schemes." One can thereby appreciate the ways in which these schemes differ and then try to assess combinations of features that seem to instill depositor confidence so as to eliminate bank runs and yet contain the resulting moral hazard that arises when depositor discipline is substantially, if entirely, eliminated.[56]

---

[56] In this regard, see Hovakimian, Kane and Laeven (2002), and Demirgüç-Kunt and Detragiache (2001).

Approximately one third of all countries have already established deposit insurance schemes. Information on selected design features for the schemes in 55 representative countries is presented in Table 6.[57] It is quite clear from this information that there are important differences in key features across all these countries, which includes both emerging market economies and mature economies. Moreover, the vast majority of these countries have only recently established deposit insurance for banks. Indeed, 44 percent of the countries have established their schemes within the past 20 years, and half of those countries established a deposit insurance scheme within the past decade. Even more countries, moreover, are either in the process or likely in the near future to establish a deposit insurance scheme.

One key feature of any deposit insurance scheme is the coverage limit for insured depositors. The higher the limit the more protection afforded to individual depositors. But the higher the limit, the greater the moral hazard.[58] The limits vary quite widely for countries, ranging from a low of $1,096 in Poland to a high of $125,000 in Italy. For purposes of comparison, the limit is $100,000 in the U.S. One problem with these comparisons, however, is that there are wide differences in the level of per capita income among these countries. It is therefore useful to compare the coverage limits after expressing them as a ratio to GDP per capita. Doing so one finds that Peru has the highest ratio at 9, whereas most of the other countries have a ratio at or close to 1. Clearly, ratios that are high multiples of per capita GDP are more likely to reduce the degree of discipline that depositors impose on banks.

---

[57] For recent and comprehensive information, see Demirgüç-Kunt and Sobaci (2001). Also, see Coburn and O'Keefe (2003).

[58] The highest "coverage," and therefore the highest degree of moral hazard, arises under systems without an explicit deposit insurance scheme, but where depositors and bankers believe there is "implicit" full coverage for all deposits by the government.

In addition to coverage limits, countries also differ in whether coinsurance is a part of the deposit insurance scheme. This particular feature, when it is present, means that depositors are responsible for a percentage of any losses should a bank fail. Only 16 percent of the countries have such a feature. Yet, to the extent that depositors bear a portion of any losses resulting from a bank failure, they have an incentive to monitor and police banks. Usually, even when countries adopt coinsurance, the percentage of losses borne by depositors is capped at 10 percent. Even this relatively small percentage, however, may be enough to attract the attention of depositors when compared with the return they can expect to earn on their deposits, and thereby help to curb moral hazard.

Some countries have elected to establish an ex-ante funded scheme, whereas others have chosen to provide the funds for any losses from bank failures ex-post. Of the 55 countries, only 13 percent have chosen to establish an ex-post or unfunded scheme. In this case the funds necessary to resolve bank failures are obtained only after bank failures occur. This type of arrangement may provide a greater incentive for private monitoring and policing, because everyone will know that the funds necessary to resolve problems have not yet been collected. And everyone will also know that a way to keep any funds from being collected is to prevent banks from engaging in excessively risky activities. The degree of monitoring depends on the source of funding. In this regard, there are three alternative arrangements: public funding, private funding, or joint funding. Of these sources, private funding provides the greatest incentive for private discipline, and public funding the least. Although the information is not provided in the table, only 15 percent of the countries fund their deposit insurance schemes solely on the basis of private sources. At the same time, however, only one country relies solely on public funding. Seven of the schemes that are privately funded are also privately administered and one is jointly administered. In none of the 55 countries where there is only private funding is the fund solely administered by government officials.

In addition to those design features, there are two other features that must be decided upon when a country establishes a deposit insurance scheme. One is whether premiums paid by banks for deposit insurance should be risk-based. The advantage of risk-based premiums is that they potentially can be used to induce banks to avoid engaging in excessively risky activities. This would give banking authorities an additional tool to contain moral hazard. Yet, in practice it is extremely difficult to set and administer such a premium structure. Table 8 shows that slightly less than one third of the countries have chosen to adopt risk-based premiums. Most countries that have adopted the schemes are careful to refer to them as differential premia systems rather than risk-based, and a common critique is that the difference between the lowest premium and the highest is quite limited.[59]

The last feature to be discussed is the membership structure of a deposit insurance scheme. A country must decide whether banks may voluntarily join or will be required to join. A voluntarily scheme will certainly attract all the weak banks. The healthy banks, in contrast, are unlikely to perceive any benefits from membership. If this happens, the funding for resolving problems will be questionable for both ex-ante and ex-post schemes. Indeed, the entire scheme may merely become a government bailout for weak banks. By requiring all banks to become members, the funding base is broader and more reliable. At the same time, when the healthy banks are members, they have a greater incentive to monitor and police the weaker banks to help protect the fund.

---

[59] Moreover, in the United States, which does have a differential premium, no premium in fact has been collected for a number of years from most banks. Relevant legislation includes a feature that allows the Federal Deposit Insurance Corporation to stop all contributions, except from banks in its highest risk category, once a certain funding ratio has been reached.

Although many countries at all levels of income and in all parts of the world have established deposit insurance schemes, they have not chosen a uniform structure. The specific design features differ widely among countries as indicated in Table 6. The fact that so many countries around the globe have suffered banking crisis over the past 20 years has generated a substantial amount of research focusing on the relationship between a banking crisis and deposit insurance. Although this type of research is still ongoing, there are currently enough studies from which to draw some, albeit tentative, conclusions about deposit insurance schemes that help promote a safe and sound banking industry.[60] They are as follows:

- Even without a deposit insurance scheme, countries have responded on occasion to banking crises with unlimited guarantees to depositors. An appropriately designed scheme that includes a coverage limit many be better able to serve notice to depositors as to the extent of their protection and thereby enable governments to avoid more costly ex-post bailouts.

- The design features of a deposit insurance scheme are quite important. Indeed, recent empirical studies show that poorly designed schemes increase the likelihood that a country will experience a banking crisis.

- Properly designed deposit insurance schemes can help mobilize savings in a country and foster overall financial development. Research has documented this important linkage but emphasizes that it only holds in countries with a strong legal and regulatory environment.

- Empirical research shows that market discipline is seriously eroded in countries that have designed their deposit insurance schemes with a high coverage limit, an ex-ante fund, the government being the sole source of funds, and only public officials as the administrators of the fund.

- Empirical research shows that market discipline is enhanced significantly in countries that have designed their deposit insurance schemes with coinsurance, mandatory membership, and private or joint administration of the fund.

---

[60] See Hovakimian, Kane and Laeven (2002); Kane (2000); Demirgüç-Kunt and Kane (2002); Demirgüç-Kunt and Detragiache (2001, 2000, 1998b, and 1998a); Demirgüç-Kunt, Detragiache and Gupta (2000); and Barth, Caprio and Levine (2003).

IV.E. Corporate Governance in Banking

Although all countries regulate and supervise banks, and many countries have instituted deposit insurance systems to promote banking system safety and soundness, a fundamental conflict remains between the owners of banks and the managers and directors of banks. The "principal-agent" problem as it has come to be known starts from the premise that the goals of owners (the principals) may be significantly different from the objectives of managers and directors (the agents), who may pursue policies inconsistent with share value-maximization. To some extent such conflicts of interest can be addressed by contractual solutions. However, high transactions costs prohibit contracts from being written to cover all possible deviations from value-maximizing behavior. Hence, additional rules and practices – "corporate governance" procedures – have been instituted to address gaps in contractual specifications of rights and obligations of the various claimants on firm value.

The issue of corporate governance for banks is particularly important, as Caprio and Levine (2002) and Macey and O'Hara (2003) argue. Banks and other financial intermediaries themselves exert corporate governance on firms, both as creditors of firms and, in many countries, as equity holders. Indeed, as Caprio and Levine (2002) point out, in many countries, especially developing ones, where banks dominate as financial intermediaries, banks are among the most important sources of governance for firms. To the extent banks are well-managed, the allocation of capital will occur efficiently in an economy. However, if there is poor corporate governance of banks, "bank managers may actually induce firm managers to behave in ways that favor the interests of bank managers but hurt overall firm performance."[61] This in turn can hurt the performance of the economy. Indeed, Bushman and Smith (2003) make an explicit

---

[61] Caprio and Levine (2002, p. 18).

connection between corporate governance of financial intermediaries and the finance-and-economic-growth literature.

Despite the importance of this issue, "very little attention has been paid to the corporate governance of banks."[62] However, in the wake of recent well-publicized governance scandals at multinational firms headquartered in the U.S. and elsewhere, there has been a renewed interest in research on corporate governance, and this interest seems in part to have stimulated new interest in research on corporate governance for banking.[63] Conceptually, Macey and O'Hara (2003) argue that given the special nature of banking, it is worthwhile to consider as "stakeholders" constituents beyond shareholders.[64] Because banks' liabilities, especially to depositors, play such a crucial role in the economy, Macey and O'Hara argue that "bank directors should owe fiduciary duties to fixed claimants as well as to equity claimants."[65] In a complementary vein, Caprio and Levine (2002) explain that there are four sources of governance for banks: "equity holders, debt holders, the competitive discipline of output markets, and governments."[66] Each of these constituents therefore has an interest in effective corporate governance for banks.

Empirically, Adams and Mehran (2003) have identified important differences between banking holding companies (BHCs) and nonfinancial firms in key characteristics of

---

[62] Macey and O'Hara (2003, p. 91). See also Caprio and Levine (2002, p. 18), and Adams and Mehran (2003, p. 123).

[63] See Shleifer and Vishny (1997) for a comprehensive and thoughtful survey of research on corporate governance. Macey and O'Hara (2003) discuss the emerging literature on corporate governance for banks.

[64] See Corrigan (1982) on why banks are considered "special." Kwan (2001) provides a concise essay on this topic.

[65] Macey and O'Hara (2003, p. 102). Adams and Mehran (2003, p. 124) add at least one more constituent. They argue that "the number of parties with a stake in [a financial] institution's activity complicates the governance of financial institutions. In addition to investors, depositors and regulators have a direct interest in bank performance."

[66] Caprio and Levine (2002, p. 19).

governance.[67] These differences extend to the size and composition of boards of directors, the structure and activities of boards, chief executives' compensation and direct equity holdings, and dispersion of ownership of company shares.

An important dimension of corporate governance is the degree of transparency that exists for the operations of a firm. The more comprehensive and accurate is information about how managers conduct the firm's business, the more effective can stakeholders be in monitoring managers' performance. Extending recent work by Caprio and Levine (2002), Table 7 presents cross-country information on bank operations transparency: (1) the effectiveness of external audits of banks; (2) the transparency of bank accounting practices; and (3) the evaluations by external rating agencies and incentives for creditors of the bank to monitor bank performance. An index summarizing country-specific component data on each of these three dimensions of corporate governance in banking is calculated, with higher values indicating better corporate governance measures.[68] In addition, the far right-hand column aggregates these indexes into a "Corporate Governance Index." As in the case of other cross-country information presented

---

[67] As they explain, because public information on governance procedures is generally available only for publicly traded bank holding companies, the holding companies are examined instead of banks. Adams and Mehran also discuss the relatively small number of other recent empirical studies of corporate governance in banking.

[68] Details of the calculations of the indexes are: The Strength of External Audit index adds one for an affirmative answer to each of the following questions: 1) Is an external audit required?; 2) Are auditors licensed or certified?; 3) Do supervisors receive a copy of the auditor's report?; 4) Can supervisors meet with auditors without prior approval by the bank?; 5) Are auditors legally required to report bank misconduct to supervisors?; 6) Can supervisors take legal action against external auditors? The Bank Accounting Transparency index adds one for an affirmative answer to each of the following questions: 1) Are financial institutions required to produce consolidated accounts covering all bank and any nonbank financial subsidiaries?; 2) Are off-balance sheet items disclosed to the public?; 3) Must banks disclose their risk management procedures to the public?; 4) Are bank directors legally liable if information disclosed is erroneous or misleading? In addition, this index adds one for a negative response to the following question: Does accrued, though unpaid interest or principal enter the income statement while a loan is still nonperforming? The External Ratings and Creditor Monitoring index adds one for an affirmative answer to the following question: Is subordinated debt allowable or required as a part of capital? The index also adds one if the top 10 banks in the country are rated by an international credit rating agency. The Corporate Governance Index is the sum of these component indexes.

throughout this chapter, the 55 countries compared in Table 7 show a relatively wide range of differences across corporate governance characteristics.

Looking at averages for the four country income groups, there is a positive relationship between the composite Corporate Governance Index and country income level. In particular, the overall (lower) Corporate Governance Index is statistically significantly lower for the lower income countries as compared with the highest two income groups.[69] With little variation in reported external audit practices, this pattern is due in part to significant differences across the country income groups in the index of bank accounting practices transparency. The index calculated to capture the degree to which external ratings agencies provide information about bank operations and performance, plus whether subordinated debt is counted as part of bank capital – with an affirmative answer increasing the likelihood that bank bond holders have a strong incentive to monitor bank performance – also accounts for part of the overall statistical significance of the positive relationship between country income level and good corporate governance procedures.[70]

V. Banking Crises

V.A. Incidence of Banking Crises

Banking crises have occurred in various countries and at various time periods throughout history. An unprecedented number, however, occurred during the last two decades of the twentieth century. More specifically, Caprio and Klingebiel (2003) have identified 117 episodes of systemic banking crises that occurred in 93 countries and 51 episodes of borderline crises that

---

[69] Statistical significance measures are not shown in Table 7. A difference of means tests shows that the Corporate Governance Index is statistically significantly different at the 99 percent confidence level for the low income group relative to the high income group, and at the 95 percent confidence level for the low income group relative to the Upper Middle Income group.

[70] Difference of means test results across each index are available from the authors upon request.

occurred in 45 countries during this time period. This means that more than half of the approximately 220 countries in the world experienced full-blown or borderline banking crises in the relatively short span of 20 years. As Figure 2 show, these crises occurred, moreover, in countries at all levels of economic development and in all parts of the globe.[71]

The worst aspect of banking crises is that they can be quite costly to resolve and disruptive to economic activity. Indeed, as Figure 3 indicates, the direct cost of resolving insolvent banks can be extremely high. The banking crises in Southeast Asia that began in the summer of 1997, for example, imposed costs of 27 percent of GDP in the case of South Korea, a still higher 33 percent in the case of Thailand, and an enormous 50 percent in the case of Indonesia. Such huge costs create enormous budgetary problems and lead to the diversion of scarce resources from more productive uses. This results in slower economic growth and development than would otherwise occur. High costs to resolve banking crises may even contribute to social unrest and the overthrow of governments, as occurred in Indonesia following its financial crisis in 1997.

V.B. Causes and Prevention

Banks are by their nature fragile firms. The reason is that they specialize in providing short-term liquidity services while simultaneously providing longer-term credit services. This maturity imbalance subjects them to potential troubles in the event that shifts in one side of the balance sheet will not be compensated by shifts in the other side. Banks are actively involved in determining what happens to their balance sheets. At times, they may deliberately attract more deposits by offering higher rates than their competitors and then extend credit for excessively risky projects promising still higher rates of return. The incentive to engage in such behavior is

---

[71] For recent and comprehensive survey on banking crises and, more generally, systemic risk, see De Bandt and Hartman (2000).

that limited liability exposes the owners of banks to the loss of only their contributed equity capital. When the amount of such capital is relatively low and when owner liability is limited to this capital, banks have an incentive to engage in excessively risky activities strategies, because the upside gain could be quite large compared with the smaller downside loss. This situation is exacerbated in the presence of generous deposit insurance schemes, because depositors have no incentive to constrain or to monitor the bank's use of their funds. Instead, this role becomes the responsibility of bank regulators and supervisors. They must impose discipline on banks, so that banks do not engage in imprudent behavior. This can be done through regulations limiting specific activities deemed to be too risky and various supervisory practices that identify and correct management or operational weaknesses. When the regulatory and supervisory authorities do not fulfill their responsibilities, the results can be disastrous.[72]

Some argue that the regulatory and supervisory authorities in many of the countries that experienced banking crises during the past 20 years did not take appropriate and timely action. Some of the international lenders to banks and firms in specific countries, for example, may have believed that the International Monetary Fund (IMF) would come to the rescue of those countries if there were a banking or other financial crisis. More funds than otherwise therefore flowed into those countries considered likely candidates to receive IMF support were a crisis to occur. Regulatory and supervisory authorities must take into account the fact that the IMF does indeed provide funds to countries experiencing crises, just as they should when a bank belongs to a deposit insurance system. Market discipline is severely weakened in such cases, if not entirely

---

[72] In this regard, Hovakimian, Kane and Laeven (2002, p.23) find that "…recent adopters of insurance have done a particularly poor job of replacing the depositor discipline that explicit insurance displaced."

eliminated. Although regulatory and supervisory discipline becomes extremely important in those situations to prevent imprudent bank behavior, it has not always been imposed.[73]

Another factor that contributes to banking crises is that some states either own banks or direct banks to provide credit to various government-owned or government-sponsored investment projects. This was the situation in some countries in Southeast Asia that experienced banking crises in 1997. In Indonesia a large percentage of banking system assets were controlled by state-owned banks. In South Korea the government simply directed that banks extend credit to fund specific projects. Such government intervention clearly reduces, if not eliminates, market discipline. This, in turn, typically leads to the inefficient allocation of resources. At the same time, such intervention can cause both domestic and foreign market participants to conclude that the government will never let banks fail. This can cause more funds to flow into banks than would otherwise occur, even when the funds are being used for excessively risky purposes. This is particularly troublesome, because in the presence of such government intervention it is unclear how the bank regulatory and supervisory authorities can promote 'safe and sound' banking practices, unless they are truly independent from the government.[74]

It is also possible for adverse shocks to contribute to banking crises. A foreign-exchange rate movement, for example, that is unforeseen and large could significantly and adversely affect economic growth, especially in small, open economies. This shock could limit the ability of firms to repay bank loans. Banks could then become insolvent if the ability of firms to repay loans deteriorates enough. Even the collateral backing such loans may turn out to be insufficient

---

[73] For an assessment of the IMF, see Meltzer (1999).

[74] See, for example, Barth, Caprio and Levine (2003); Barth, Brumbaugh, Ramesh and Yago (1998); La Porta, Lopez-de-Silanes and Shleifer (2002); and Corsetti, Pesenti and Roubini (1998).

to prevent bank insolvencies as it decreases in value along with the general slowdown in economic growth resulting from the adverse shock.

Banking crises are obviously caused by a variety of factors. Bank runs, adverse shocks, and moral hazard can all contribute to banking crises – not to overlook bad luck, mismanagement, and downright fraud. No matter what causes crises, governments can take actions that precipitate as well as exacerbate them. Financial liberalization, for example, in an environment in which banks are inadequately capitalized and bank regulation and supervision are weak is a recipe for disaster. Also, allowing inadequately capitalized banks to grow rapidly is unwise. As banks grow rapidly, for instance, they may make real estate loans and accept real estate as collateral for the same loans. This can contribute to a real estate bubble that creates a banking crisis when it bursts. Indeed, the most frequently found common denominator in studies of banking crises around the world throughout history is imprudent and speculative real estate lending. Banking crises can therefore occur more frequently and be more costly when governments fail to impose the discipline on banks that private market participants would impose. In this sense, bank regulation and supervision matter for stability in the banking sector.

In recent years there has been a rapidly growing number of studies of banking crises.[75] This interest has been fueled by the large number of costly banking crises in recent years. But it is also fueled by the increasing availability of data necessary to analyze these crises. Based upon this data, studies have been conducted by academics and by researchers at both central banks and multinational agencies. Much more research must be conducted to understand more fully the

---

[75] See, for example, Aggarwal (1999); Boyd, Gomis, Kwak and Smith (2001); Caprio and Klingebiel (1996 and 1999); Demirgüç-Kunt and Detragiache (1998a, 1998b and 2000); Eichengreen and Arteta (2000); Frydl (1999); Gourinchas, Valdes and Lenderretche (2001); Hardy and Pazarbşioğlu (1999); Hutchison and Neuberger (2002); Kaminsky and Reinhart (1999); Lindgren, Garcia and Saal (1996); Kho and Stultz (2000); McKinnon and Pill (1998); Rojas-Suarez and Weisbrod (1996); and Barth, Caudill, Hall and Yago (2000).

nature of banking crises. Despite this situation and the fact that banking crises can never be completely preventable, there are several actions that countries can take to lessen the likelihood of their occurrence and to reduce their costs should they occur.[76]

First and foremost, all available evidence indicates that high inflation and sluggish real economic growth significantly increase the likelihood of a banking crisis. High real interest rates have also been found to be associated with systemic banking sector problems. This means that countries must pursue macroeconomic policies that prevent an environment of high real interest rates, high inflation, and recessions, and thereby lessen the likelihood of a costly banking crisis.

Second, banks always have an incentive to engage in excessively risky activities because they are highly leveraged firms operating with limited liability. This situation is exacerbated when banks also operate with access to a generous deposit insurance scheme. To control the risk-taking proclivity of banks, bank regulatory and supervisory authorities must be sure that banks operate in a safe and sound manner. This is not an easy task. Banks must not be regulated so tightly that they are unable to adapt to a changing financial marketplace. This would only weaken them and provide a greater incentive to engage in excessively risky activities in an attempt to improve profitability. At the same time, banks must not be so loosely regulated that they are able to use risk-free deposits to fund all types of activities with little regard to the associated downside losses. This balancing act has resulted in banks being regulated and supervised differently across countries with varying degrees of success.

The important point is not so much the length of the checklist of regulations and supervisory practices, but rather how to keep in check the incentive to engage in excessively risky behavior. Providing appropriate incentives to banks should be the ultimate goal of bank regulation and supervision. In addition, market participants must have both the information and

---

[76] See, for example, Bisignano, Hunter, and Kaufman (2000), Borio (2003) and Kaufman (2000).